cool collectibles

STAMPS

Jennifer Abeyta

HIGH interest books

Children's Press
A Division of Grolier Publishing
New York / London / Hong Kong / Sydney
Danbury, Connecticut

Book Design: Michael DeLisio
Contributing Editors: Rob Kirkpatrick and Mark Beyer

Photo Credits: Cover, p.37 © Corbis; p.5 © H.D.Thoreau/Corbis; p.6 © Hulton-
Deutsch Collection/Corbis; p. 8, 14, 16, 18, 19, 20, 21, 28, 33, 34, 41 by Dean
Galiano; p.11 © Mitchel Gerber/Corbis; p.17 © Patrick Ward/Corbis; p18 ©
Archive Photo; p. 24 © Uniphoto; p. 30 © Jennie Woodcock; Reflections
Photolibrary/Corbis.

Visit Children's Press on the Internet at:
http://publishing.grolier.com

Library of Congress Cataloging-in-Publication Data

Abeyta, Jennifer.
    Stamps / by Jennifer Abeyta.
    p. cm. – (Cool collectibles)
    Includes bibliographical references and index.
    Summary: Explains how to begin a stamp collection, including information
    on the history and value of stamps.
    ISBN 0-516-23334-3 (lib. bdg.) – ISBN 0-516-23534-6 (pbk.)
    1. Postage stamps—Collectors and collecting—Juvenile literature. [1.
    Postage stamps—Collectors and collecting.] I. Title. II. Series.

HE6213.A23 2000
769.56—dc21

                                                          00-026217

Contents

Introduction

Do you like to learn about exciting historical events? Would you like to know more about important people in history? Do you enjoy learning about other countries? Do you like art and design? If you answered "yes" to any of these questions, stamp collecting might be a great hobby for you.

Stamps have been made in the United States for more than 150 years. Stamps have colorful and interesting designs. They are also educational. The pictures on stamps have celebrated generations of athletes, historical events, inventions, musicians, presidents, and scientists.

Before you start collecting, you should learn as much as you can about the subject of stamps. There are millions of stamps out there. Today, each country makes its own stamps. Some

Stamps come from all around the world.

stamps are harder to find than others. Some are worth a lot of money.

Stamp collectors have been around almost as long as stamps themselves. Almost anywhere you go, you can see other collectors' stamps at auctions, hobby shops, flea markets, and collector shows. As you start your own collection, remember that it is your collection. From start to finish, you have the freedom to decide how, when, and what to collect.

Enjoy your new hobby!

Why Stamps?

New stamps come out all the time. The United States Postal Service (USPS) makes stamps. Then the USPS sells stamps so that people can use them for mail. But many people consider stamps to be works of art. They collect stamps because of the interesting designs on them. People who collect stamps are called philatelists.

WHAT ARE POSTAGE STAMPS?

Postage stamps are small, square or rectangular pieces of paper. They have a picture on the top and a sticky glue on the bottom. You need postage stamps to send letters through the mail. First, you must buy stamps at a post office. Then,

Stamps are made in uncut sheets. Later, they are cut into individual stamps.

Stamp designs have pictures of famous people, inventions, and the natural world.

before you put your letter in the mailbox, you affix (stick on) a stamp or stamps to an envelope by moistening the sticky side of the stamp. If a stamp is self-stick, it can be peeled off its backing and affixed to envelopes without moistening it. The stamp tells the postal delivery person that you have paid money to the USPS. Your mail will not be delivered unless you have affixed the right amount of postage.

The amount of postage you must use for each piece of mail depends on the weight of the envelope or package. The heavier the mail, the more postage you have to use. Because mail can be either very light or very heavy, the USPS makes stamps that are worth different amounts. The postal values of individual stamps range from one cent to several dollars. The value of the stamp is always printed in one of its corners.

The actual rate of postage is decided by the government. Every few years, the government raises the price of postage. Then, the USPS has to make new stamps to keep up with the new postal rates.

TYPES OF STAMPS

There are many new designs on stamps every year. It is easy to get lost trying to keep track of all the different stamps that are out there.

Definitives

Some stamps issued by the USPS have designs that do not celebrate a specific, time-dated event or person. They may have designs with patriotic themes, such as an American president or the U.S. Capitol building. These stamps are called definitives. The USPS issues definitives for a long time to meet ordinary postal rates. Usually, definitive stamps are sold to the public for several years. Definitives also are known as regular issue stamps.

Commemorative Stamps

The USPS also makes stamps that celebrate special people, places, or events. Such stamps are called commemorative stamps. Often, these kinds of stamps are issued on the anniversary of a person or event. The USPS usually makes them in limited quantities for only a few months. Collectors rush to buy commemorative stamps before they sell out.

Dave Thomas and Rosie O'Donnell were at the first day ceremony for the "Building a Home" stamp.

OTHER POSTAL COLLECTIBLES

Anything that people like to collect is a collectible. Stamps are not the only collectibles of interest to philatelists. They collect other items that the USPS sells, such as postcards, stamped envelopes, and items that commemorate the first day of a new stamp issue.

First Day Collectibles

On the day the USPS introduces a new stamp design, it holds a first day ceremony at a special location. For example, the USPS held a first day ceremony at the Kennedy Space Center to celebrate the issue of the thirty-three-cent Space Shuttle stamp. Collectors like to get their hands on items from first day ceremonies. The USPS makes special envelopes that bear the brand-new stamps. They are called first day covers. The USPS also makes programs for these ceremonies. A new stamp is attached to the program. You receive a program when you attend a first day ceremony.

DID YOU KNOW?

The smallest stamp ever produced was a South American stamp from the 1860s, which was 0.31 inches by 0.37 inches (7.9 mm by 9.4 mm). The largest-ever stamp was a Marshall Islands stamp that was 6.3 inches by 4.33 inches (16 cm by 11 cm), issued in 1979.

Countries throughout the world print their own stamps. Canada issues a number of commemorative stamps every year. The designs of these stamps celebrate different aspects of Canadian life. In 2000, the Canadian postal service issued stamp designs to celebrate Canadian birds, the nation's tourist attractions, and its national holiday, Remembrance Day.

The ten-cent George Washington stamp issued in 1847

The History of Stamps

The British government issued the first postage stamps in 1840. These stamps had a picture of Queen Victoria on them. Before the U.S. government issued stamps, city postmasters sold their own stamps, called postmaster provisionals. They were used in St. Louis, New York, and a number of other cities. Today, postmaster provisional stamps are very rare. They are very valuable to collectors.

THE FIRST AMERICAN STAMPS

In 1847, the U.S. government issued postage stamps for the first time. They issued more than 3.7 million red-brown stamps that featured a picture of Benjamin Franklin, the nation's first postmaster general. These stamps were worth five cents each. The government also issued nearly 900,000 copies of a black, ten-cent stamp with a  picture of George Washington. Both the Franklin and Washington stamps had gummed backs. However, sheets of these stamps did not come with small holes outlining the stamps (perforations). The sheets had to be cut, folded, or torn so that people could use individual stamps. These early stamps are called imperforates. Perforated stamps didn't come out until ten years later. Imperforate stamps are highly valuable to collectors.

POPULAR POSTAGE

The government did not know whether people would like using stamps. However, it became

Stamp collectors like to build their collections.

clear that stamps were popular with the public. Some people even bought stamps and saved them. This was the beginning of stamp collecting. The first known stamp-collector's album (storage book) was published in 1862.

COLORFUL MEMORIES

In 1869, the U.S. government issued a series of stamps that had pictures of inventions or

Early stamps celebrated events such as the
Pony Express and the landing of Columbus.

events, rather than people. These were the first commemorative stamps. The subjects of these stamps included the Pony Express, the locomotive, the signing of the Declaration of Independence, and Christopher Columbus's landing in America.

These stamps were also the first multicolored stamps. To make these stamps, workers ran sheets through two separate presses. The first press printed a frame and the postage value of each stamp in one color. These sheets were allowed to dry. Then the second press printed the design of each stamp in a different color.

Oops!

It took some time for workers to learn this process. Sometimes, they fed sheets into the second press upside-down. This mistake produced some stamps with upside-down designs. These upside-down stamps became known as invert stamps. To prevent invert stamps, the government added  control steps in the process to make sure that they would not make any more inverts.

Flying Upside-Down

In 1918, 100 sheets of a new stamp design were issued. This design was a picture of the Curtiss Jenny single-engine airplane. On the day these stamps came out, a stamp collector named William T. Robey bought a sheet in Washington, D.C. When he looked closely at the sheet, he

The famous inverted Jenny

noticed that the airplane design was upside-down. Robey was very excited with his new find!

When the U.S. government found out about Robey's sheet, it was embarrassed. It offered to buy back the sheet, but Robey refused. Pretty soon, collectors everywhere tried to buy the sheet of inverted Jennys from Robey. Finally, he sold them to a collector from Philadelphia for $15,000. Later that year, a collector in New York bought the sheet and broke them into blocks (groups of four stamps). Today, a single inverted Jenny stamp is worth more than $50,000.

TWENTIETH-CENTURY STAMPS

More and more stamps came out in the late 1800s and the 1900s. Some stamps celebrated national parks, such as Yellowstone and Yosemite. Others featured designs for individual states. In 1937, a new set of stamps featured pictures of the American presidents. The postage value of each of these stamps matched the order of the president it pictured. For example, a picture of the sixteenth president, Abraham Lincoln, was on the sixteen-cent stamp. Other stamps commemorated such

events as the building of Hoover Dam and the 1939 World's Fair.

Stamp designs became much more complex toward the middle of the century. Advances in production machinery allowed workers to make stamps with three or more colors. In 1957 and 1958, the Champions of Liberty eight-cent stamp series featured pictures of world leaders, using red, white, blue, and gold. Some of the most colorful stamps in the twentieth century commemorated endangered species, the conservation movement, and the Olympic games.

DID YOU KNOW?

Several unique (only one made) stamps have been issued throughout the world. They are highly collectible. The most famous unique stamp is the one-cent black and magenta stamp issued by British Guyana in 1856.

A COMPLETE COLLECTION

In the last half of the twentieth century, a collector named Robert Zollner decided that he wanted to collect at least one of every U.S. stamp ever made. This was not going to be an easy task. To complete his collection, he would have to go to collector shows and auctions throughout the country. He would have to find stamps that had not been used for more than a century. Some of these stamps were worth a lot of money. Zollner would have to spend a lot of time and money to finish his collection.

It took Zollner fifteen years, but eventually he achieved his goal. After he completed his collection, Zollner exhibited it twice to the public. The collection included the rarest U.S. stamp, a one-cent stamp from 1868. Zollner also had other rare stamps, including one of the inverted Jennies. In October 1998, Zollner sold the entire collection at an auction for $8.3 million!

The Value of Stamps

Philatelists collect stamps for different reasons. Some collect rare stamps. Others collect stamps that have designs they like. Others collect stamps that commemorate people whom they admire. Some philatelists even like to collect stamps and other postal items from foreign countries.

Some stamps are worth more to collectors than are other stamps. Besides the subject of the stamp design, a number of other factors determine the value of a stamp. A major factor that determines a stamp's value is its condition.

Stamp collectors use special tools to handle their stamps.

25

CONDITION

Collectors like to find stamps that are still in good condition. Stamps that look as new as the day they first were issued are in high demand among collectors. The colors of the design are sharp and clear. The edges are straight with no rips or tears. These stamps are described as "mint." Very old stamps that are still in (or close to) mint condition are considered great finds.

The condition of a stamp also is determined by other factors. These factors include centering, gumming, and cancellation marks.

Centering

When stamps are perforated, stamp makers try to center the stamp design within the perforation marks. Stamps do not always come out perfectly, though. In some cases, the perforation marks cut into the stamp design. The most prized stamp usually will have a perfectly centered design.

Gumming

Sometimes, a stamp's gumming wears off. Other stamps may lose their gumming if they are handled sloppily. A mint stamp still has the same gum that it did on the day the stamp was issued.

Cancellation

When someone uses a stamp to send mail, the post office stamps an ink pattern on the stamp. This pattern is called a cancellation mark. When a stamp is canceled, it cannot be used again.

Collectors usually like to find stamps that were never used. First day covers are exceptions to this practice. First day covers come with cancellation marks that indicate the date and location of the ceremony.

If a stamp has been canceled, the darkness of the cancellation ink can affect the stamp's popularity among collectors. Stamps with cancellation marks that are light are more popular than stamps with heavy or smeared cancellation

Some stamp designs are mistakenly printed upside down.
Error stamps such as this one are valuable to collectors.

marks. The difference is that a light cancellation mark allows the stamp's design to be seen more easily.

ERRORS, FREAKS, AND ODDITIES

Although some collectors like to get stamps that are perfect, others like to find stamps that show mistakes which happened during production. A stamp may have missed a step in production, or it may have undergone steps that were done incorrectly. This type of stamp is called an error. A stamp also may have had a partial mistake in production, such as a smeared or crooked design. This is called a freak stamp. Finally, a stamp might have an odd design or an unusual mistake, such as the design of another stamp printed on its reverse side. This kind of stamp is called an oddity. Stamps such as these can be popular with collectors because usually they are very rare.

DID YOU KNOW?

The stamp with the lowest-ever postal value was issued by Hungary in 1946. It was worth three hundred pengo in Hungarian money. At the time, one American cent was worth 604.5 trillion pengo.

Starting Your Own Collection

Are you ready to start collecting stamps now? Great—let's begin! Don't know where to start? Where can you find stamps? What do you do with stamps when you've got them?

Relax. The key to collecting is that there are no rules. Collecting is a hobby. The only thing you need to do is to have fun. Pick the types of stamps you want to collect. Figure out the best places to find them. Then decide how you want to protect and display them.

WHERE TO BUY STAMPS

You can buy U.S. stamps from any post office. This is the easiest way to find new stamps. Most

Beginning collectors have fun deciding how to display their stamps.

post offices advertise the different stamps that they sell.

If you are looking for old stamps, you can look for them in a number of different places. Some stores specialize in selling stamps and other collectibles. A number of Internet auctions have listings from people who want to sell their stamps. Look in newspapers and magazines for dealer and auction ads. Check out some flea markets. Or find a stamp collector's club and share your interest with others.

FINDING FREE STAMPS

If you do not mind collecting used stamps, there are a number of great ways to add to your collection. Begin by asking all of your friends and relatives to save stamped envelopes for you. Just have them toss used envelopes in a box for you instead of in the wastepaper basket. If you would like to collect foreign stamps, go to a local travel agency and ask them if they have

An easy way to get stamps is from
letters that your friends send you.

any used envelopes. Or you can start writing to
a pen pal from another country. Whenever your
pen pal mails you a letter, you will get a stamp
or stamps from his or her country on the envelope. One of the best things about finding
stamps in this way is that it costs you only the
price of a stamp to send your own letter!

Collectors are careful when they
remove stamps from envelopes.

REMOVING STAMPS FROM ENVELOPES

If you get a used envelope, you might want to
remove the stamp so that you can put it in an
album. Removing a stamp can be tricky. You
need to be very careful if you do not want to
tear the stamp or ruin the gumming.

First, cut or tear the envelope around the
stamp. Make sure you don't tear the stamp itself!

Place it stamp-side down in a small container of warm water. If you want to remove more than one stamp at a time, make sure the bowl is big enough. You don't want the stamps to stick to each other.

Let the stamp float in the water. Wait until the gum dissolves. The stamp will slide off the paper. Lift the stamp out of the water with tongs. Be careful! Wet stamps are very fragile. Place the stamp between two paper towels. Let it dry overnight. The next day, your stamp may be curled. Don't worry. Put the stamp inside a thick book, such as a dictionary or telephone book. After a few days, the weight of the book's pages will have flattened the stamp.

Drying New Stamps

Some newer stamps have gum that is invisible. If you are working with newer stamps, it will be hard to tell when all of the glue dissolves from their backs. Let these stamps dry facedown with nothing touching the gum side. Otherwise, the stamps might stick to something while drying. You can press and flatten these stamps after they dry.

PHILATELIC FREEDOM

Once you begin your collection, you need to figure out how to store your stamps. There are many methods for storing stamps. If you are not concerned with the value of stamps, you may be happy keeping them in a shoebox or cigar box. The choice is yours!

TOOLS FOR THE COLLECTOR

As you start to build your collection, you will need certain things to help you handle and protect your stamps. As most hobbies do, stamp collecting has its own tools. These tools include a pair of tongs, some hinges or mounts, and a stamp album. Take a look at all of the different tools and decide which ones work for you.

Tweezers and magnifying glasses
are tools used by philatelists.

Tongs

Tongs are metal tools that look like tweezers. However, tongs have special ends that are good for picking up delicate items such as stamps. If you use tweezers to pick up a stamp, you might scratch the stamp's surface. If you don't mind minor scratches, then tweezers are fine. Do not use your fingers to pick up stamps. In time, the oil from your skin can damage a stamp.

Hinges

Many collectors like to put their stamps in special stamp albums. To put stamps in these albums, many collectors use thin, transparent (see-through) pieces of paper that are resistant to air and grease. This type of paper is called glassine. Collectors put stamps on pieces of glassine paper called hinges. One side of the hinge is moistened and affixed to the back of the stamp. The other side of the hinge is moistened and affixed to the page of a stamp album. Hinges are cheap and very popular with collectors, especially collectors of canceled stamps. However, collectors who like unused stamps or mint stamps tend not to use hinges. Once you attach a stamp to a hinge, it is no longer considered to be in mint condition.

Mounts

Some collectors do not want to stick hinges (or anything else) onto their stamps. If this concerns you, you can pay more money and buy mounts. A mount is a case that encloses the stamp. The face of a mount is clear, and the background is usually black or dark blue. You can place a stamp in the mount. Then, you can stick the mount onto an album page.

Albums

Most collectors put their stamp collections in albums. Some albums come with pictures and information about the many different stamps that have been issued throughout the years. When you get a stamp, you place it over its picture in the album. Some collectors like this type of album because it shows them all kinds of stamps they might find. Other albums come with blank pages. Blank pages allow the collector to arrange stamps however he or she wishes.

Starter Kits

Are you starting out as a stamp collector and do not want to spend a lot of money? You might want to buy a starter kit. These beginner kits usually have tongs, some hinges, a magnifying glass, and a booklet about stamp collecting. A kit also may include some stamps. Most likely, these stamps will not be rare or valuable.

SELLING YOUR STAMPS

Many collectors enjoy finding popular, valuable stamps. If you put together a valuable collection, you may want to sell it at some point in the future. You can sell stamps at the same places where you can buy them: collectible stores, auctions, shows, stamp club meetings, or on the Internet.

If you want to get an idea of how much your collection is worth, you should take a look at postage stamp price guides such as *Blackbook*, *Scott's Standard Postage Stamp Catalogue*, and *Linn's Stamp Market Index*. Price guides list the possible values of a stamp, based on stamp condition. However, keep in mind that dealers

The *BlackbookPrice Guide* for the year 2000

pay less than these prices when they buy your stamps. Then they can resell them later at the stamps' list prices and make a profit. Still, it can be fun to look through price guides to see how many different kinds of stamps are out there.

New Words

affix stick on

album a book used to store a stamp collection

auction a sale at which items are sold to the highest bidder

block an unseparated group of four stamps, two high and two wide

cancellation a mark placed on a stamp to show it has been used

centering how well the design of a stamp was placed within its margins

commemoratives stamps that honor important people, places, events, inventions, or things in nature

condition the physical state of a stamp; the way a stamp is graded for determining its value

definitives regular postage stamps, issued for long periods of time

error a stamp that is either missing a part of its production or has a major error

first day cover an envelope with a new stamp

New Words

and cancellation showing the date on which the stamp was issued

freak a stamp that issues with a minor error, such as a fold or crease, too much ink, or a color missing

glassine thin, transparent paper that is resistant to air and grease

gum glue on the back of a stamp

hinge a strip of transparent paper by which stamps are placed in an album

imperforate stamps without perforations

mount a sturdy case in which stamps are placed in an album

perforations small holes between stamps that make them easy to separate

philatelist stamp collector

postmaster general the person in charge of the nation's postal service

sheet a number of stamps printed together but not yet cut into individual stamps

tongs a tool shaped like tweezers that is used to handle stamps

unique only one made

unused a stamp that hasn't been used for mail; not canceled

used a stamp that has been used for mail; canceled

For Further Reading

Books

Datz, Stephen R. *Stamp Collecting*. Loveland, CO: General Trade Corporation, 1999.

Granger, Neill. *Stamp Collecting*. Brookfield, CT: Millbrook Press, 1994.

Grossman, Samuel, and Chuck Adams. *Start Collecting Stamps*. Philadelphia: Running Press Book Publishers, 1996.

Hudgeons, Marc, and Tom Hudgeons. *The Official 2000 Blackbook Price Guide to United States Postage Stamps*. New York: The Ballantine Publishing Group, 1999.

Melkowski, Yvonne M., and James Criswell. *Is Stamp Collecting the Hobby for You?* Kansas City, MO: Truman Publishing Company, 1998.

Organizations

American Philatelic Society (APS)

P.O. Box 8000

State College, PA 16803

814-237-3803

Web site: *www.west.net/~stamps1/aps.html*

The internationally recognized society for stamp collecting in the United States.

Junior Philatelists of America

P.O. Box 021164

Brooklyn, NY 11202-0026

Web site: *www.jpastamps.org*

This is a site for the association for beginning collectors.

United States Postal Service

Web site: *www.usps.com*

The official site of the USPS.

Index

Index

About the Author

Jennifer Abeyta lives with her husband and three children in Oceanside, California. Stamp collecting is a passion that she has passed onto her children. She has found that collecting stamps is a great way to bring the family together.